ADDICTED
to Social Media

Carla Mooney

ReferencePoint
Press®

San Diego, CA

© 2020 ReferencePoint Press, Inc.
Printed in the United States

For more information, contact:
ReferencePoint Press, Inc.
PO Box 27779
San Diego, CA 92198
www.ReferencePointPress.com

LIBRARY OF CONGRESS CATALOGING-IN-PUBLICATION DATA

Names: Mooney, Carla, 1970– author.
Title: Addicted to Social Media/by Carla Mooney.
Description: San Diego, CA: ReferencePoint Press, Inc., [2019] | Series:
 Addicted | Audience: Grade 9 to 12. | Includes bibliographical references
 and index.
Identifiers: LCCN 2019016237 (print) | LCCN 2019017775 (ebook) | ISBN
 9781682825747 (eBook) | ISBN 9781682825730 (hardback)
Subjects: LCSH: Social media—Juvenile literature. | Social media
 addiction—Juvenile literature. | Social media—Security
 measures—Juvenile literature.
Classification: LCC HM742 (ebook) | LCC HM742 .M657 2019 (print) | DDC
 302.23/1—dc23
LC record available at https://lccn.loc.gov/2019016237

Contents

Looking for Likes

Since its introduction, social media has exploded in popularity. In 2005, about 5 percent of Americans used social media. Compare that to the nearly 70 percent of Americans who, according to the Pew Research Center, were on at least one social media platform in 2018. Social media sites such as Facebook, Twitter, Instagram, and Snapchat have become an integral part of communication, allowing users to connect with each other and create a sense of community.

For many Americans, social media is part of their daily lives. About 74 percent of Facebook users, 63 percent of Snapchat users, and 60 percent of Instagram users report that they visit these sites at least once a day. Although young adults were the early adopters of social media, today's social media users are more representative of the general population. Young people continue to use social media at a high rate, but an increasing number of older adults have set up profiles in recent years. Across the United States, the most widely used social media site in 2018 was Facebook, but other sites, such as Twitter, Pinterest, Instagram, and LinkedIn, were also popular among Americans.

Social media has many positive attributes. It connects people to new ideas and new people in new places. It allows people to share work and cultures across geographic borders. For many, it makes the world a smaller, more connected place.

Increasing Use Sparks Rising Concerns

Despite the positive impact social media use can have, concerns have emerged about the amount of time people spend on these sites. Elizabeth Stinson, a journalist who writes about design, technology, and science, admits that she mindlessly burns hours on social media, often without intending to do so. "Most of the time, I navigate to my social media apps reflexively, as though my finger and the icons are magnets. I don't even realize I'm doing it until my thumb taps the Instagram icon on my screen. Again. And again. And again," she says. "It's a dirty digital habit, and it doesn't make me happy. Maybe you can relate. Studies have repeatedly found that while social media connects us to one another, it also makes us feel bad. And yet, we do it anyway. We do it because we can't stop."[1]

When it comes to spending time on social media, how much is too much? The answer varies from person to person. What is manageable for one person may cause a problem for another. In addition, many users underestimate the time they spend online. When they track their social media use, the results are often eye-opening. Reporter Hayley Sewell was shocked when she checked her usage levels. "I look at mine nearly 100 times every day. That's once every 15 minutes," she says. "That includes the seven hours a night that I sleep so I actually check it every 10 minutes when I'm awake." Like many people in their twenties, Sewell constantly kept her phone within reach, so she could check it at any time. "But I never saw a problem—until now," she says. Sewell says that she often finds herself sucked into a social media black hole, moving from one platform to the next, scrolling endlessly for new content. "By the time I'm back around to the beginning, enough time has passed for new content, and so it continues. It's a dangerous cycle, especially before bed," she says. Sewell believes that her use of social media has crossed into dependence. "I've never smoked but I imagine I'm addicted to social media like smokers crave nicotine. I've resolved to cut back but I'm honest enough to know that I couldn't stop completely,"[2] she admits.

> "I've never smoked but I imagine I'm addicted to social media like smokers crave nicotine."[2]
>
> —Hayley Sewell, a reporter and social media user

Frequency of Teen Social Media Use

The frequency that teens use social media is surging. Although the proportion of teens who use social media has not changed significantly, 83 percent in 2012 compared to 81 percent in 2018, the frequency of their social media use has spiked substantially. In 2012, only 34 percent of teens checked social media more than once a day. In 2018, that number skyrocketed to 70 percent. The increase in social media frequency is causing concerns that more teens are at risk of developing a social media addiction.

Frequency of Social Media Use, 2012 vs. 2018

Among all 13- to 17-year-olds, percentage who check social media

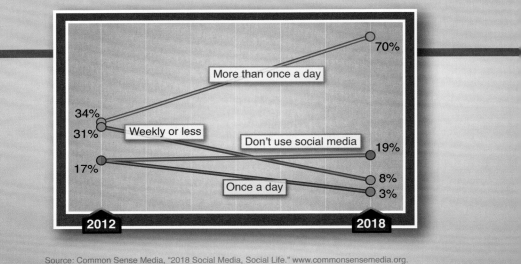

More than once a day — 70%

34%
31% — Weekly or less

Don't use social media — 19%

17%

Once a day — 8%
3%

2012 — 2018

Source: Common Sense Media, "2018 Social Media, Social Life." www.commonsensemedia.org.

The Impact of Excessive Use

What is the impact of spending hours a day on social media? While the sites are too new to fully understand the long-term effects they may have, several negative effects on users' health and well-being have already been linked to excessive social media use. For some people, constantly focusing on social media can impact their physical health, cause eye damage, and disrupt their sleep. Others experience anxiety, depression, and lower self-esteem. An intense focus on social media can also damage personal relationships with family and friends, as users become more distant and distracted, unable to focus on anything outside of their online world. Understanding the impact of excessive social media use is especially critical for young people, who are some of the most enthusiastic users of this technology.

Many people are able to enjoy social media without a problem. However, when social media users find that their use is damaging their real-life relationships and compromising their performance at work or school, it might be time to realize they have a problem.

What Does It Mean to Be Addicted to Social Media?

As of 2018, approximately 3.1 billion people—roughly one-third of the world's population—used social media. Some users, however, seem to spend nearly every waking moment on their phone. They constantly check multiple social media accounts and scroll endlessly through feeds. They furiously like posts and pictures, comment on news stories, upload details about their latest adventures, and tweet about hot topics. But some people have a difficult time finding the right balance when it comes to social media. They begin to spend so much time online that it starts to take over their lives.

Defining an Addiction

Being addicted to social media is different than being addicted to drugs or alcohol; after all, there is no chemical substance that causes one's body to become physically dependent on social media. Instead, those who are addicted to social media have what is known as a behavioral addiction, similar to what happens when a person uncontrollably gambles or shops. Such behavior is compulsive, meaning that the person feels compelled to perform it despite the negative toll it may take on his or her life. Over time, the compulsion to engage in these activities begins to take over, interfering with other important activities such as work or school.

Given this, a social media addict is someone who uses social media excessively and in a compulsive way. The social media addict is not content to check Facebook or Instagram occasionally. Instead, he or she compulsively checks news feeds and statuses for so many combined hours that it begins to cause serious problems.

Teen Samantha Matt knows that she spends too much time on social media. She wastes hours of her day checking LinkedIn, browsing Pinterest, looking at Snapchat, scrolling through Instagram, and updating and refreshing Twitter and Facebook. She checks all of her accounts immediately upon waking up, and she continues to scroll through them as she gets ready for her day. She refreshes her feeds while stopped at red lights in the car, and "once I'm at work or school, I plug into my social networks on my desktop." She continues to check in with her accounts throughout the day. "If I have to go to the bathroom, I bring my phone. On quick coffee runs, I obviously bring my phone. I've got my phone in class and panic when I see notifications go off that I cannot check because I am in a meeting,"[3] she says. The only place she does not check her social media is during her daily workout.

She ends each night by checking her phone, and she often has trouble falling asleep because she develops anxiety over not checking social media. Matt knows that she has a problem. "It's an addiction to social media. It's an addiction to being plugged in, or in other words, a fear of NOT being plugged in," she says. "If I went offline, I could probably interact with real live humans for an additional 6 hours each day."[4]

> "It's an addiction to being plugged in, or in other words, a fear of NOT being plugged in."[4]
>
> —Samantha Matt, social media user

The Demographics of Social Media Addiction

Matt is not alone in her overuse of social media. According to Mediakix, an influencer marketing agency, the average person spends almost two hours per day on social media. Teens may spend up to nine hours a day on such sites. Increasingly, much of that time is spent on the go, another factor that contributes to social media's overuse. Worldwide, 2.9 billion people actively use mobile devices like smartphones and tablets to access social media, anywhere and at any time. Of these users, researchers estimate more than 210 million may suffer from Internet and social media addictions.

Just because a person uses social media, however, does not mean they will become addicted. In fact, many people are able to manage their social media use without a problem. According to a 2018 Pew Research Center social media study, less than half of Americans who use social media (40 percent) believe it would be hard to give up social media, with only 14 percent saying that

Being addicted to social media is a behavioral addiction, meaning that there is no chemical substance that causes one's body to become physically dependent on it.

it would be very hard. However, the number of people who think they have a problem is growing. When researchers polled Americans in January 2014 on the same topic, only 28 percent of social media users said it would be hard to give up social media, and just 11 percent said it would be very hard.

So what affects whether someone becomes addicted to social media? Age is one factor; young adults report feeling more attached to social media than do older adults. In the same 2018 Pew study, 51 percent of social media users ages eighteen to twenty-four said it would be difficult for them to give up social media. In comparison, only one-third of users ages fifty and older felt that giving up social media would be hard.

Along with age, gender may also be a factor in who becomes addicted to social media. In a 2017 study, researchers from Norway and the United Kingdom surveyed more than 23,500 people about their social media habits. They investigated the demographic, personality, and individual differences associated with social media addiction and found that young, single females are more likely to become addicted to social media than any other demographic group. Researchers also discovered that having low self-esteem and displaying narcissistic traits (that is, being self-absorbed) also increased a person's likelihood of becoming addicted to social media. People with low self-esteem and narcissism come to crave the instant feedback they receive on their posts; it serves to boost their self-importance and self-worth. Researchers suspect that people with low self-esteem or narcissism may be drawn to social media and use it excessively because these platforms "fulfill a need for affiliation and confirm the sense of an idealized self."[5]

Not Officially Recognized as a Disorder

Although awareness is growing about these problems, mental health professionals do not currently classify social media addiction, a subset of a broader problem known as Internet addiction, as specific disorders. In the 2013 *Diagnostic and Statistical*

Manual of Mental Disorders, the authoritative guide that medical professionals use to diagnose mental disorders, Internet addiction is listed as a "condition for further study." This is because researchers who have studied Internet use and mental health do not agree on whether excessive time spent on the Internet and social media platforms should be considered an addictive behavioral disorder.

Some argue that reports of social media addiction are mostly anecdotal. They believe that more scientific research on the subject is needed before an official disorder can be established. "The question of whether or not disordered online social networking use can be considered a 'true' addiction is a tough one," says psychologist Julia Hormes. "I think the answer really depends on your definition of 'addiction.' Many people think of addictions as involving ingested substances."[6] Yet others, like Mark Griffiths at Nottingham Trent University in England, believe that behaviors that center around some kind of reward—such as what the brain feels when a person satisfies their compulsion to check social media—can be considered addictive. "Do I believe that people can be so engrossed in social media that they neglect everything else in their life?" says Griffiths. "I do."[7]

> "Do I believe that people can be so engrossed in social media that they neglect everything else in their life? I do."[7]
>
> —Mark Griffiths of Nottingham Trent University

Concerns Are Driving New Research

As researchers consider whether social media addiction should be an official disorder, they have continued to study the effects of social media use. Some studies have found evidence that excessive Internet and social media use has similarities to drug and alcohol addictions.

In a 2017 study, for example, researchers at Swansea University in the United Kingdom and Milan University in Italy found that excessive Internet use may result in physical changes. Scientists

followed 144 participants, ages eighteen to thirty-three, as they used the Internet. They measured the participants' heart rates and blood pressure before and after they went online, and they assessed their anxiety levels and self-reported Internet dependency. Participants who excessively used the Internet had a higher heart rate and blood pressure after using the Internet, and they reported having increased feelings of anxiety. Participants who did not use the Internet excessively did not experience changes in heart rate, blood pressure, or anxiety levels. "We have known for some time that people who are over-dependent on digital devices report feelings of anxiety when they are stopped from using them, but now we can see that these psychological effects are

The Bergen Facebook Addiction Scale

In Norway, researchers have developed the first-ever scale to measure whether a person is addicted to Facebook. The Bergen Facebook Addiction Scale measures problem behavior linked to Facebook use and is based on six criteria. According to an article on the *Medical News Today* website, participants respond to each of the following criteria by responding either (1) very rarely, (2) rarely, (3) sometimes, (4) often, or (5) very often:

1. You spend a lot of time thinking about Facebook or planning how to use it.

2. You feel an urge to use Facebook more and more.

3. You use Facebook in order to forget about personal problems.

4. You have tried to cut down on the use of Facebook without success.

5. You become restless or troubled if you are prohibited from using Facebook.

6. You use Facebook so much that it has had a negative impact on your job/studies.

If a person scores "often" or "very often" on at least four criteria, it suggests he or she may have a Facebook addiction.

Quoted in Catharine Paddock, "Facebook Addiction—New Psychological Scale," *Medical News Today*, June 22, 2015. www.medicalnewstoday.com.

accompanied by actual physiological changes,"[8] says professor Phil Reed of Swansea University, who led the study. According to the study's authors, these physical changes and increased anxiety are similar to the withdrawal symptoms experienced from drugs such as alcohol, cannabis, and heroin. "These results seem to show that, for some people, it is likely to be an addiction,"[9] says professor Roberto Truzoli of Milan University, a coauthor of the study.

A different study by researchers at Michigan State University in 2019 showed that excessive social media users often exhibited poor decision making, similar to what occurs in drug and alcohol addicts. "Decision making is oftentimes compromised in individuals with substance use disorders. They sometimes fail to learn from their mistakes and continue down a path of negative outcomes," says the study's lead author, Dar Meshi. "We investigated this possible parallel between excessive social media users and substance abusers."[10]

In the study, the team surveyed seventy-one participants about their psychological dependence on Facebook. Questions included how preoccupied they felt with Facebook, how they felt when they could not use it, if they had attempted to quit social media, and the impact Facebook had on work or school. The participants then performed tasks that measured their decision-making skills. The researchers found that participants who made bad decisions were the ones who often used social media excessively. This result shows that excessive social media use is associated with an inability to make good decisions in high-risk situations. A similar trait has been observed in people who have substance abuse disorders. "I believe that social media has tremendous benefits for individuals, but there's also a dark side when people can't pull themselves away," says Meshi. "We need to better understand this drive so we can determine if excessive social media use should be considered an addiction."[11]

> "I believe that social media has tremendous benefits for individuals, but there's also a dark side when people can't pull themselves away."[11]
>
> —Dar Meshi, a researcher at Michigan State University

Signs of Social Media Addiction

Although social media addiction is not officially recognized as a disorder by health professionals, it can significantly disrupt a person's life. People who are addicted to social media often display signs of obsessive or compulsive behavior pertaining to these sites. They spend a lot of time thinking about the content on social media sites or fantasizing about using them. People who are addicted to social media feel an urgent need to share or post. Sometimes, this results in sharing more personal details than they should, which can later cause them to regret what they posted.

Over time, the irresistible urge to tweet, check a status, or scroll through a feed grows more and more frequent. Users constantly check for social media updates whenever they have a free moment. They leave social media sites open on their phone or computer so they can check every few minutes, even when working on school assignments or professional tasks.

Turning to social media to forget about real-world personal problems can be another sign that someone has a social media addiction. A person suffering from relationship problems or who is having difficulties at school or work may temporarily turn to social media to reduce their stress. However, constantly diverting one's attention to social media means they invariably spend less time solving their problems in a productive and healthy manner.

Many social media users check for updates whenever they have a free moment. Oftentimes, this fixation distracts users from doing homework or other important responsibilities.

Duplicate Accounts

Not only are many teens spending hours on various social media platforms, but some have multiple accounts on the same platforms, which causes them to spend even more time online. According to Common Sense Media's 2018 report on teen social media use, about 16 percent of social media users say they have multiple accounts on the same platform. Typically, teens set up duplicate social media accounts to hide the content they post from parents or use them for interacting with a select group of close friends.

On Instagram, many teens have a second account called a "finsta," which is a combination of the words *fake* and *Instagram*. Often, they use their finsta to post different content than they post on their main account. Many teens say that although their main Instagram account is carefully edited, their finsta is more intimate and authentic. They might post a bad selfie or an emotional rant that they would never put on their main account. Esther Choi, a seventeen-year-old from Suwanee, Georgia, says that she only posts on her real Instagram account "the best parts and the big, good parts of my life." She adds, "On my finsta, it's the good, the bad and the ugly. It's a more multifaceted version of me." Keeping up with all of these accounts is another factor driving excessive social media use in some teens.

Quoted in Taylor Lorenz, "The Secret Instagram Accounts Teens Use to Show Their Realest, Most Intimate Moments," Mic, May 3, 2017. https://mic.com.

People who are addicted to social media experience a form of withdrawal when they are unable to access their accounts. For example, when in a place that lacks cell phone service, people who feel addicted to social media can become anxious, restless, and depressed until they are able to access their social media accounts again. Withdrawing from social media can trigger feelings of irritability and boredom, along with strong cravings to go online.

One of the most telling signs that a person has a social media addiction is that it begins to negatively affect their relationships. They increasingly use social media to communicate, and it becomes their primary medium for sending messages, sharing photos, and engaging with other people. Eventually, they become more comfortable communicating online than in real life. They also spend hours online, passively scrolling through feeds. Social media use turns addictive when a person is online so much that they have less time to hang out with friends and family or enjoy other activities.

Social media marketer Jason Thibeault quit Facebook over his concern that he had developed an addiction. He explained his decision in a blog post, saying, "As a writer, speaker, and marketer, I knew that digital [media] played an important role in my livelihood and career. But it got to the point where the digital updates that were furiously filling my news feeds were becoming an addiction. They were a constant interruption pulling me away from the work that I was otherwise enjoying."[12] Since quitting Facebook, Thibeault says he feels liberated from the need to constantly check his news feed and "like" status updates.

Although it is not an official disorder, social media addiction is a very real problem for many people. The constant need to go online, scroll through feeds, and compulsively check activity consumes more and more of their time. Eventually, this addiction has a real-world impact, crowding out other interests and taking away time with friends and family.

Why Is Social Media So Addictive?

Some people doubt that social media can be addictive because it is inherently different from drugs, alcohol, or other habit-forming substances that people typically ingest. Yet millions of people feel dependent on social media; they become anxious and fearful when they cannot go online, and they center their lives around their ability to use these platforms. For them, social media use can turn addictive.

An Innate Desire to Be Social

Social media sites are not inherently addictive. When using social media, there is nothing users put into their bodies that makes them come back for more. What is addictive about these sites is the all day, every day social environment they provide. Especially when used on smartphones and other mobile devices, Facebook, Snapchat, Instagram, Twitter, and other platforms give users access to an enormous social environment that they can carry in their pocket anywhere they go.

The human species is hardwired to be social. Scientists have learned that connecting with other humans is an important part of survival and evolution. According to psychology professor Matthew Lieberman of the University of California, Los Angeles, the need to connect socially with other humans is as basic as the need for food, water, and shelter. "Mammals are more socially connected than reptiles, primates more than other mammals, and humans more than other primates," says Lieberman. "Becoming more socially connected is essential to our survival."[13] Lieberman suggests that the human need to be social may explain why people feel the urge to interact on social media.

Brain Chemicals Drive Our Need to Be Social

The human desire to be social is reinforced by brain chemistry. Using social media affects the human brain, causing it to release two chemicals that play a role in addiction: dopamine and oxytocin. Dopamine is involved in motivating behavior. It drives the human feelings of want and desire, which leads people to seek out and search for substances and behaviors that provide satisfaction and happiness. "Dopamine is our brain's way of recording what's worth doing again," says Ramsay Brown, the cofounder and chief operations officer at Boundless Mind, a tech start-up that investigates how the brain's dopamine system can be used to encourage positive behaviors. "It's how we learn from our positive experiences."[14]

> "Dopamine is our brain's way of recording what's worth doing again. It's how we learn from our positive experiences."[14]
>
> —Ramsay Brown, the cofounder and chief operations officer at Boundless Mind

However, dopamine cannot help the brain tell the difference between a healthy habit and an unhealthy one. As a result, dopamine plays a role in many addictions. Addictive drugs such as amphetamines, cocaine, and heroin affect the brain's dopamine system by causing it to release more dopamine than usual. These drugs also hinder a person's ability to resist impulses. Therefore, the more a person uses, the more dopamine his or her brain releases. In turn, the desire to do things that provide satisfaction becomes harder to resist. "These unnaturally large rewards are not filtered in the brain—they go directly into the brain and overstimulate, which can generate addiction," says Wolfram Schultz, a professor of neuroscience at Cambridge University. "When that happens, we lose our willpower."[15]

The human species is hardwired to be social. This primal need to connect with others may explain why people feel the urge to interact on social media.

Using social media can also flood the brain with dopamine. Every time someone finds something new or exciting on their social media feed, the brain releases dopamine. This tells the brain that checking social media is a behavior worth repeating. In this way, every notification, like, tweet, or share has the potential to trigger the release of dopamine, which reinforces the cycle.

Social media also causes the brain to release oxytocin. Known as the cuddle chemical, oxytocin generates feelings of love, trust, empathy, and generosity. According to 2013 research from Stanford University, any type of social connectivity triggers the release of oxytocin. Oxytocin, in turn, causes the release of the neurotransmitter serotonin, which activates the brain's reward circuits to generate happy feelings. In one experiment, researchers found that spending ten minutes on Twitter raised the brain's oxytocin levels as much as 13 percent—the same amount as some people experience on their wedding day.

Together, dopamine and oxytocin create a loop that keeps users on social media. Dopamine starts users seeking, and oxytocin rewards them for the behavior, making them want to repeat it over and over again. This loop of want and reward makes it difficult to stop a behavior—in this case, tweeting, liking, commenting, and otherwise using social media.

The nature of social media makes this loop even more addictive. Consider that the brain is stimulated to release dopamine when unpredictable things occur. Social media is inherently unpredictable; users never know what the latest tweet, comment, or like will pertain to, what it will say, or who it will be from. Dopamine is also sensitive to cues that signal a reward is coming. When a user's phone beeps or dings to indicate they have an update on Facebook, the sound becomes a cue that triggers the dopamine system. Similarly, social media's short bursts of information are

Intermittent Variable Rewards

Social media sites pull in users by using a strategy known as intermittent variable rewards. To understand this concept, imagine playing a slot machine. A person pulls the lever and waits with anticipation while the pictures or numbers spin. Eventually, the reels slow and a random picture or number falls into place on the machine. Winning or losing is decided by which pictures line up with the pay line on the viewing window. In this scenario, pulling the lever is what is known as an intermittent action. It is linked to what is called a variable reward—the player may win (or may not). The variable reward keeps players hooked and brings them back for more.

Social media also uses intermittent variable rewards to keep users coming back. When a user opens Instagram or Facebook, it often takes a few seconds to load updates. That is not an accident. Those few seconds of delay make the site feel variable. Will there be an update? Did someone send a message or like a post? Each time they refresh, users do not know what they will "win." The anticipation keeps them coming back for more.

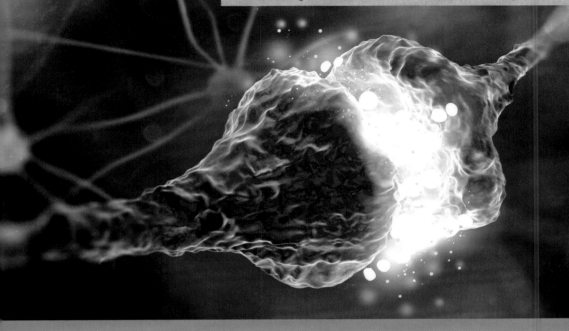
Dopamine, a naturally occurring "feel-good" chemical in the brain (white area), is released by neurons to the receptors of nearby neurons. Using social media can flood the brain with dopamine.

powerful stimulants to the dopamine system. When information comes in short bites, such as 140 characters on Twitter, it does not fully satisfy users. It therefore triggers the release of dopamine to motivate them to seek more satisfaction. All of these factors make it harder for users to resist the pull of social media.

The Brain's Reward Centers

Scientists can use neuroimaging studies to clearly identify the areas of the brain that become activated when someone engages with social media. In a 2016 study, researchers at the UCLA brain mapping center used a functional magnetic resonance imaging (fMRI) scan to image the brains of teens as they used a custom social media app that resembled Instagram. An fMRI scan measures brain activity by tracking changes associated with blood flow. In the study, the teens were shown more than 140 images while researchers identified the areas of their brain that became active when the teens liked posts.

Push Notifications

Sometimes even the smallest, most insignificant features can have a big impact on social media users. When asked what feature he thinks manipulates social media users the most, Justin Rosenstein, a former Facebook employee, points to the simple push notification.

A push notification is a message that pops up on a smartphone or other mobile device. It tells the users that there has been an update in their social media feed—someone may have commented on their post, shared a photo, or liked their status. Users might be in the middle of something else, but a push notification causes their phones to beep, alerting them of new activity. Typically, they will stop what they are doing, pull their phones out, open a social media app, and respond. "The vast majority of push notifications are just distractions that pull us out of the moment," Rosenstein says. "They get us hooked on pulling our phones out and getting lost in a quick hit of information that could wait for later, or doesn't matter at all." Push notifications also take advantage of users' social impulses. Once they get an alert that someone has liked their post or they have unread messages and notifications, they feel social pressure to respond.

Quoted in Julian Morgans, "Your Addiction to Social Media Is No Accident," Vice, May 19, 2017. www .vice.com.

The scans showed that the nucleus accumbens, part of the brain's reward circuit, was more active when the teens saw that their photos had received a lot of likes. This positive reaction could, in turn, cause them to use social media more often. "When teens learn that their own pictures have supposedly received a lot of likes, they show significantly greater activation in parts of the brain's reward circuitry," says lead author Lauren Sherman. "This is the same group of regions responding when we see pictures of a person we love or when we win money." Sherman suggests that these results could explain why teens are so likely to use social media. "Reward circuitry is thought to be particularly sensitive in adolescence," says Sherman. "It could be explaining, at least in part, why teens are such avid social media users."[16]

Social Media's Psychological Pull

Humans love to talk about themselves. In fact, studies show that the average person spends about 30 to 40 percent of all speech talking about themselves. When it comes to online communication, that percentage is even higher. Social media draws users in by giving them an easy way to talk about themselves. In just a few clicks and keystrokes, they can share photographs of a recent event, give updates about their vacation plans, or brag about their accomplishments. Moreover, they can set their messages to reach their entire social network at any time, from any place.

Perhaps even more appealing to users, social media allows them to polish their self-presentation. When interacting face-to-face, it can be difficult to hide one's flaws or disappointments. Online, however, users are able to present only the image they want others to see. They can select a profile photo that highlights their favorite physical features. They can edit posted photos using flattering filters and software like Facetune, which further eliminates the natural flaws and blemishes that all people have. They can share achievements and awards while never mentioning the failures or troubles they have encountered.

Viewing a carefully crafted positive image of oneself can even pump up a person's own self-esteem. Research has shown that people experience a spike in good feelings about themselves after viewing their own social media profile. By crafting their online image to reflect their best traits, users are reminded of what they like best about themselves. "It's like the way you might feel good about yourself when you check yourself out in the mirror before a date,"[17] explains Amy Gonzales, an assistant professor who studies social media and health at Indiana University's Media School.

Sharing the right content can also improve a person's social currency. Social currency is anything one shares that makes others like them more. Posting the right picture, update, or news triggers positive reactions from others and increases a person's perceived popularity. How many likes did a photo get on Instagram or Facebook? How many retweets did a post get on Twitter? The more positive engagement people receive on what they post on social media, the better they feel about themselves and the more popular they and others perceive themselves to be.

The Fear of Missing Out

For some users, the fear of missing out, also known as FOMO, drives their addiction to social media. People share information on social media twenty-four hours a day, seven days a week. While the constant influx of information can make people feel connected, it can also put pressure on users to constantly check or post to their accounts, lest they miss out on being the first to know the latest news.

One teen's experience highlights the extent to which FOMO factors into social media's strong pull. In 2017 Sheveen, a teen from England, tried to give up all social media for a week, as an experiment for school. At first, he thought it would be easy, but he underestimated the grip social media had on him. "As we shut off our devices, I already felt as if I had lost a limb," says Sheveen. He stayed offline for a few days before finally breaking down and checking his accounts. "The thought of all the messages coming through at the weekend, and plans that I wanted to know about, made me worry about what I was missing out on. It all weighed down on me. It was too much. I broke."[18]

"As we shut off our devices, I already felt as if I had lost a limb."[18]

—Sheveen, a British teen who tried to give up social media for a week for a school experiment

Making Social Media Irresistible

Social media sites actively work to keep their users online. The modern world is filled with many things competing for people's time and attention, and social media sites are aware of this. In fact, such sites rely on getting people's attention; getting attention is at the core of their business model. The more attention a site draws, the more effective its advertisements will be, which brings in lucrative revenue to the company that owns the site.

Social media companies use a number of tactics to make their sites interesting and engaging so that people are reluctant to stay away from them. One prime example is the like button, which Facebook introduced in February 2009. At first, it seemed like a pretty simple idea. Users could click the thumbs-up button to show they liked another Facebook user's post. Although the like button seems harmless, it actually has a downside. "The like button, simple as it was, tapped into a bottomless font of social feedback,"[19] explains Adam Alter, the author of *Irresistible: The Rise of Addictive Technology and the Business of Keeping Us Hooked*.

Facebook first introduced the "like" button to keep users more engaged. The feature also fulfilled some users' need for social validation.

Following Facebook's lead, YouTube adopted a like/dislike feature in 2010, and Instagram followed by unveiling its heart-shaped button. In 2015 Twitter adopted the heart-shaped button as well. These features all reflect the fact that social media platforms recognize their users' need for social validation; they make social media sites more engaging and increase the amount of time and attention users devote to them.

From 2006 to 2010, Leah Pearlman worked for Facebook and was one of the coinventors of the site's like button. She admits that this feature led her to become hooked on the site. She began measuring her self-worth on the basis of the number of likes she received on her posts. After a while, she realized she was checking social media for many reasons, many of which were negative. "When I need validation—I go to check Facebook," she says. "I'm feeling lonely, 'Let me check my phone.' I'm feeling insecure, 'Let me check my phone.'. . . Suddenly, I thought I'm actually also kind of addicted to the feedback."[20]

Snapchat's streak feature is another example of a social media site's efforts to keep users online and engaged. A streak is the number of consecutive days two users have exchanged snaps. The site displays the number next to each person on a user's friend list. For many Snapchat users, keeping multiple streaks becomes an obsession. Users send out snaps each day simply to keep those streaks going, and many brag about their longest streaks. When on vacation or otherwise unable to regularly access their social media accounts, some users even give their site passwords to a friend who can keep their streaks going until they return. "It's clear here that the goal—keeping the streak alive—is more important than enjoying the platform as a social experience,"[21] says former Google designer Tristan Harris.

Designed on Purpose?

Some people do not think that that social media companies set out to design features that would become addictive to users. "I don't think social media companies are trying to make 'addictive' platforms, per se," says Alter. "But since they're all competing for our (limited) time and attention, they've always been focused on making the most engaging experience possible."[22] Others disagree, arguing that these companies have deliberately added features to their sites to hook users and keep them coming back for more. In 2006 Aza Raskin, a leading technology engineer, designed the infinite scroll—one of the features on many social media sites that is believed to be highly habit forming. Using infinite scroll, users can endlessly swipe through a news feed or content without clicking or reaching a natural break at the end of a page. Raskin says the feature keeps users looking at sites much longer than they otherwise would. "If you don't give your brain time to catch up with your impulses, you just keep scrolling,"[23] he says.

Raskin explains that the designers behind social media sites are incentivized to create addictive features; the more time users spend on a site, the higher the site's stock price climbs or the more advertising dollars it is likely to pull in. "Behind every screen on your phone, there are . . . literally a thousand engineers that have worked on this thing to try to make it maximally addicting,"[24] he says. Sandy Parakilas, a former Facebook employee who worked at the company for seventeen months, agrees. "There was definitely an awareness of the fact that the product was habit-forming and addictive," he says. "You have a business model designed to engage you and get you to basically suck as much time out of your life as possible and then [the site is] selling that attention to advertisers."[25]

Social media platforms are meant to be engaging and entertaining. A variety of factors explain why users are drawn to social media, including the human need for social activity, human brain chemistry, and the way in which sites are designed. However, these factors can cause some people to become addicted to social media.

> "Behind every screen on your phone, there are . . . literally a thousand engineers that have worked on this thing to try to make it maximally addicting."[24]
>
> —Aza Raskin, technology engineer

Chapter Three

How Do People Become Addicted to Social Media?

No social media user intends to develop an addiction upon first creating an account. However, an increasing number of people are becoming dependent on these sites. This type of addiction is called a behavioral addiction; it occurs when people become dependent on and crave a set of behaviors, regardless of the impact they have on their lives.

Addicted to a Behavior

Behavioral addictions are exactly what they sound like—behaviors that a person is compelled to perform over and over again. Being addicted to a specific behavior causes a person to crave doing the behavior, lack the ability to stop, and feel compelled to continue even though it negatively impacts their lives. Any behavior could turn addictive if it provides a person with a reward and feelings of pleasure. Common behavioral addictions include being unable to stop oneself from gambling, having sex, going shopping, and looking at the Internet. Although the behavior itself is not bad, the compulsion to perform it and the inability to stop turn it into a problem.

A behavioral addiction begins the same way that a drug or alcohol addiction does. When a person performs the behavior, it creates feelings of pleasure. The brain responds to all pleasures in the same way, no matter if they come from taking a drug, winning the lottery, having a sexual encounter, or browsing the Internet. In all of these situations, the brain releases the neurotransmitter dopamine in the nucleus accumbens, which is a group of nerve cells underneath the brain's cerebral cortex. This area of the brain is called its pleasure center.

When a behavior floods the nucleus accumbens with dopamine, a person experiences an immediate rush of euphoria. When this pleasurable feeling is linked to a particular behavior, it provides a reward that makes the person experiencing this sensation want to do the behavior over and over again. This is not a problem in most people. In fact, some behaviors, like eating and sex, are necessary for human survival; reinforcing them ensures the species will continue. For some people, however, the euphoria associated with the behavior causes the behavior to become overwhelming, compulsive, and addictive. They find themselves doing the behavior more and more frequently, at the expense of other parts of their lives.

An Increased Risk

This is why not all of Facebook's 2.32 billion monthly active users or Twitter's 321 million (as of 2018) become addicted to the sites. Just like other addictions, some people are simply more vulnerable to getting hooked on social media. Scientists have not found one specific risk factor that increases a person's chance of developing a behavioral addiction. However, there are certain characteristics that may be shared by people who struggle with these addictions.

Often, people who are addicted to the Internet and social media have low self-esteem. They look for validation online, hoping to feel better about themselves. Scrolling through news feeds and seeing responses to their posts may trigger an unusually strong reward for them.

Another common characteristic is to have experienced childhood trauma or loss. Some people turn to the Internet and social media as a way to escape uncomfortable, sad, upsetting, or lonely feelings. Using social media might help them feel better for

Shopping, like using social media, can become a behavioral addiction. While the behavior itself is not bad, the compulsion to perform it and the inability to stop, turn it into a problem.

a little while or at least distract them so they do not have to think about whatever is bothering them. However, in this process, they are at risk of teaching themselves to depend on social media to cope with their feelings.

People who excessively use the Internet and social media can find themselves socially isolated. They lack face-to-face interaction with real people, which is useful for developing good communication skills and confidence. As a result, people who become addicted to digital realms tend to have poor social and communication skills. They prefer to interact behind the safety of a screen and find live environments uncomfortable. Lacking strong communication skills can also contribute to poor self-esteem, which just continues the cycle of addiction.

Hattie's Story

Hattie Gladwell turned to social media during a point in her life when she was feeling bad about herself. As a teen, she signed up for Tumblr, an online blogging platform, while she was dealing with health problems that kept her at home for a significant amount of time. "I was feeling low in myself, both physically and mentally, and I needed a distraction," she says. Hattie joined the site to post photos and take a break from watching television and studying. She did not post that much at first, but it made her feel good when she started to notice more people following her and reposting her photos. "I loved it," she says. "Online, I was so different. I was someone who was confident, I was someone who received attention and I was someone who others were actually curious about."[26]

In real life, Hattie spent much of her time at home, sick and alone. She had friends who visited and she occasionally went out, but increasingly, the best part of her night was when she got home and could log on to her Tumblr account. Even when surrounded by friends and family, she constantly checked the site, scrolled to see who had posted, and noted how many people were looking at her blog. She became obsessed with the site and went online for hours at night, repetitively scrolling through her feeds and editing posts to make her blog look inviting and attractive. Although she still felt insecure in her real life, Hattie's online persona made her appear confident and in control.

As she spent more time online, Hattie's real life suffered. She lost friends, many of whom had become tired of constantly talking about Tumblr and how many followers Hattie had. She had trouble focusing on conversations, blindly nodding at others while she scrolled on her phone. Eventually, her friends stopped inviting her out. Hattie's real-life world grew smaller and smaller as her list of social media connections grew longer and longer. Over time, Hattie found it easier to be on social media than to interact with people in the real world. She found it hard to focus, and she was

33

increasingly uncomfortable around friends. "I hated thinking about real life because it highlighted how lonely it was away from the computer,"[27] she says.

After a year of such problems, Hattie decided to quit Tumblr and focus on re-forming her real-life community. "I look back and wonder why I spent so much time trying to be this person I really wasn't to all of these people I didn't even know," she says. "I realize how self-absorbed it all seemed now. But the only reason I can really think of is self-validation, and the need to escape a life I felt miserable in, and a body that made me feel insecure,"[28] she says. Today, Hattie values her friendships and loves to spend time with others, and feels relieved to have overcome her addiction to social media.

How Much Is Too Much?

How much is the right amount of time to spend on social media? The answer is different for everyone. One person may be able to handle spending a few hours a day on such sites; another person may not be able to set a limit, and she or he may feel the need to spend more and more time online.

In 2018 BBC Future, a division of public service broadcaster BBC, conducted a Twitter poll about what people thought constituted spending too much time on social media. Among those who responded, there was little agreement. More than a third (40 percent) said that two or three hours per day was too much time to spend on social media. Yet according to statistics from the market research company GlobalWebIndex, the average Internet user spent more than two hours per day on social media and messaging services in 2017. Since the majority of those users did not have an addiction to social media, the amount of time that they spent online was not a problem for them.

Researcher Mark Griffiths, who studies behavioral addictions, explains that the amount of time spent on social media is not an accurate predictor of who will become addicted. A person who has a lot of responsibilities offline, whose time on social media impedes his or her ability to meet these obligations, may have more of a problem than someone with fewer responsibilities. "You can have two people doing things identically—it makes a big difference if someone has a job, partner and two children,"[29] he says. As long as a person's use of social media does not affect his or her job, school, or personal relationships, there is often little reason for concern. Therefore, time spent online may be just one factor in who becomes addicted to social media.

Some people turn to the Internet and social media as a way to escape uncomfortable, sad, and upsetting situations and feelings.

One social media addict who keeps her identity anonymous has blogged about her experiences and struggles in this area. In hindsight, she is not sure what made her vulnerable to becoming addicted when so many of her friends were able to use social media without a problem. For her, however, social media quickly became all-consuming.

In January 2018 she decided to join Twitter after years of resisting all social media. She built a small network of like-minded people, all of whom followed the same accounts. Soon, she realized that she could use Twitter to get breaking news, have easy access to celebrities, and learn about new products and businesses. She found it fun when new users followed her accounts. She began to spend more time thinking about her online world,

Internet Addiction

While some people are addicted to social media, others have a broader addiction to using the Internet. An Internet addiction is also a behavioral addiction, one that often involves trouble controlling one's impulses. Internet addicts form an emotional attachment to online friends and activities. They become dependent on the Internet's chat rooms, social media sites, and other virtual communities where they can meet, socialize, and exchange ideas with other users. Some spend countless hours surfing website after website. Like other addictions, a person's Internet use becomes problematic when it starts to interfere with his or her real life and replaces real human connections and interactions.

Warning signs of an Internet addiction include thinking constantly about being online, using the Internet in increasing amounts of time, and repeated unsuccessful attempts to cut down on Internet use. At-risk users may also feel restless, moody, depressed, or irritable when they cannot go online. When logged on, they frequently spend more time than they intended. They may lie to family members and friends to hide their Internet usage. For some, Internet usage has become so consuming that it causes problems with relationships, work, or school.

obsessively checking her account to see how many likes and retweets she got. "I start to feel what many people before me have felt: the highs and lows of social media. When it's good, it's good—your self-esteem is high, you're feeling well liked, and well received. And when it's low, it sucks," she says. "It started to become too much. I was turning into someone I had never thought I would be: feeling validated by the number of likes I got."[30]

Soon, her Twitter use became obsessive. She checked her account as soon as she woke up and even sometimes in the middle of the night. She checked while she was driving; she stayed logged in all day at work. "It had quickly turned from something 'neat' into something destructive," she says. "Everything I was living I was thinking could be a potential tweet. Which meant in turn, while I was physically there, I wasn't really present in my actual life." Eventually, she decided to deactivate her account completely. "Twitter didn't give me the flu or bronchitis, but it made me sick," she says. "Unhealthy. Ill-feeling. And it could have been any social media platform that did it, I just happened to have chosen Twitter."[31]

> "Twitter didn't give me the flu or bronchitis, but it made me sick. Unhealthy. Ill-feeling."[31]
>
> —An anonymous social media user

Personality Traits and Addiction

Certain personality traits may contribute to whether a person develops an addiction to social media. At Binghamton University in New York, researchers sought to learn more about what personality traits make some social media users more vulnerable to addiction. "There has been plenty of research on how the interaction of certain personality traits affects addiction to things like alcohol and drugs," says the study's leader. "We wanted to apply a similar framework to social networking addiction."[32]

In the study, the researchers asked more than three hundred college students detailed questions to learn about their social media use and their personalities. The study was based on the five-factor personality model, which has been used as a framework in psychology since the 1980s. According to the model, most human personalities are made up of varying levels of five traits: neuroticism, conscientiousness, agreeableness, extraversion, and openness to experience. The researchers wanted to see whether any of these personality traits made a person more likely to develop a social media addiction.

The team found that three of the traits—neuroticism, conscientiousness, and agreeableness—played a role in social media addiction. Neuroticism, which is how likely a person is to feel anxious and stressed, increased the chance of becoming addicted to social media. On the flip side, people with higher levels of conscientiousness, who can control impulses and achieve

The amount of time spent on social media does not necessarily indicate addiction. However, if using social media impedes a person's ability to meet their obligations, they might be addicted.

J.J. Redick Quits Social Media

Even celebrities struggle with social media addiction. In August 2018 J.J. Redick, a basketball star with the NBA's Philadelphia 76ers, quit social media. He erased all of his social media apps, including Twitter and Instagram. He deleted all of his accounts, even the private ones reserved for close family and friends.

Redick had been stuck in a cycle where he constantly logged on to social media without even thinking about it. He constantly stared at his phone, ignoring his wife and two young sons. "It's not even conscious," Redick says. "I hate to admit it, but anytime you're at a stoplight and your phone is within reach? You pick it up. It's become instinctual. Even if you put the phone down and walk out of the room, you're always aware of where it is. It's become an extension of you." Since quitting, Redick says that he feels like a burden has been lifted from him.

Quoted in Tom Haberstroh, "Is Social Media Addiction in the NBA Out of Control?," Bleacher Report, October 1, 2018. https://bleacherreport.com.

goals, were less likely to become addicted. However, when these two traits are combined, neuroticism seemed to overpower conscientiousness for social media addiction. Therefore, a person who scored highly for both traits could have stress and anxiety that overpowered self-control and put them at a higher risk for addiction.

Meanwhile, agreeableness, which measures how friendly and empathetic a person is, did not have an effect on a person's chance of developing a social media addiction all by itself. Yet when combined with conscientiousness, it did have an impact. The researchers noted that personalities with low levels of agreeableness and conscientiousness were more likely to develop a social media addiction. This was not surprising, as they had already noted that people who were not conscientious were more likely to become addicted to social media. However, the researchers were surprised to find that the opposite was also true: people with high levels of agreeableness and conscientiousness were also at a higher risk of social media addiction. These agreeable people may be more likely to be dependent on social media because they value their friendships and deliberately use social media to maintain them.

Many Factors for Addiction

There are many factors that influence whether a person becomes addicted to social media. Some people are able to manage their time online, but others become so drawn into social media that it threatens the other parts of their life. Scientists agree that more research is needed to better understand who is at risk and why. "It's a complex and complicated topic," says Isaac Vaghefi, a professor at Binghamton University who has studied personality traits and social media addiction. "You can't have a simplistic approach."[33]

Living with a Social Media Addiction

Many people say that they are addicted to Facebook or Twitter, but in reality, their use of social media has little impact on their day-to-day life. For others, however, social media has grown from an occasional habit to an addiction that takes over many aspects of their lives. There are physical, mental, and social consequences associated with being addicted to social media.

Harming Mental Health

Numerous studies have found that social media can wear on a person's mental health, putting them at risk for depression, anxiety, and lower self-esteem. In 2016 researchers at the University of Pittsburgh reported that social media use was significantly associated with increased depression in young adults. They surveyed more than seventeen hundred young adults in the United States ages nineteen to thirty-two and found that those who spent the most time per day on social media (the top 25 percent) had significantly greater odds of having depression than those who spent the least amount of time per day on social media (the lowest 25 percent). Similarly, participants who visited social media sites the most each week (the top 25 percent) were also more likely to experience depression than those who visited the sites least per week. "This study demonstrates a strong and significant association between social media use and depression,"[34] conclude the researchers. Although more research is needed to understand the impact of online interaction on mental health and depression, studies like this indicate that there is a connection between the two.

The link between social media use and depression was further examined in a 2018 study by researchers at the University of Pennsylvania. Researchers divided 140 undergraduate students into two groups to answer questions about their anxiety levels, depression, and loneliness. The first group was then told to continue using Facebook, Snapchat, and Instagram for three weeks, as they regularly would. The second group was instructed to limit their use of each platform to ten minutes per day. Across three platforms, this totaled thirty minutes daily. After three weeks, participants who limited their daily use of social media reported experiencing lower levels of depression and loneliness, especially if they had begun the study with higher depression levels. "Here's the bottom line," says study author Melissa G. Hunt. "Using less social media than you normally would leads to significant decreases in both depression and loneliness. These effects are particularly pronounced for folks who were more depressed when they came into the study."[35]

One reason why this might be the case is that comparing oneself to others on social media typically makes people feel bad. Jennifer Garam, a Brooklyn-based writer, is one person who hates how social media provides an endless opportunity to compare herself to others, and in ways that usually have poor outcomes for her mental health. "On Facebook and Twitter, everything is always wonderful for everyone and all their lives are amazing," she says. "Even if I start out feeling moderately OK about myself, by the time I get off Facebook I feel like I haven't done anything with my life," she says. She calls this game "compare and despair" for the way it makes her feel inadequate about her life. "I immediately get sucked into comparing and despairing, and lose all sense of groundedness, of being anchored to my life. Untethered, I float away from my ability to feel good about myself and my accomplishments."[36]

"I immediately get sucked into comparing and despairing, and lose all sense of groundedness, of being anchored to my life."[36]

—Jennifer Garam, a writer and social media user

42

Some studies have linked social media use to depression. Researchers also found that there is a connection between heavy social media use and feelings of low self-esteem and anxiety.

Increased Anxiety

People who are addicted to social media often struggle with anxiety. Because social media is measured in likes, follows, and retweets, it gives users "actual data on how much people like them and their appearance,"[37] says Lindsey Giller, a clinical psychologist at the Child Mind Institute. Giller thinks that having access to such data—despite the fact that it is not statistically significant (that is, scientifically useful or accurate) or even reflective of what people actually think (since many people may not like or follow someone for reasons completely unconnected to whether they actually like the person)—causes many teens to needlessly suffer from increased anxiety and insecurity, poor self-esteem, and sadness.

How Social Media Affects Very Young Children

Increasingly, children younger than ten are turning to social media to measure their self-worth. In England, researchers studied children as young as eight who use social media sites like Instagram, Snapchat, and WhatsApp. The researchers found that within just a couple of years, the children had become very aware of their online image and felt significant pressure to make their posts as popular as possible. "If I got 150 likes, I'd be like that's pretty cool, it means they like you," says eleven-year-old Aaron, a study participant.

Study author Anne Longfield comments that many of the children had begun to measure their status by how many likes they got, and they even changed their behavior in real life to promote their image on social media. Longfield cautions that children are growing up "worried about their appearance and image as a result of the unrealistic lifestyles they follow on platforms like Instagram and Snapchat, and [they are] increasingly anxious about switching off due to the constant demands of social media." This dependence on social media at such a young age—and especially using it to measure popularity and self-worth—may be may be the first step on the path to social media addiction.

Quoted in Katherine Ruston, "The Children Aged Ten Who Are Addicted to Social Media: Happiness Is Dependent on Number of 'Likes' They Get, Reveals Major Study," *Daily Mail* (London), January 3, 2018. www.dailymail.co.uk.

When Ben Jacobs, a DJ with several thousand followers on Twitter, noticed that the site was making him anxious, he decided to take a break from social media. "Twitter did indeed make me feel anxious," he says. "It slowly dawned on me I was concerning myself with the feelings of the thousands of strangers I followed, while they didn't necessarily know who I was."[38] Since taking time off from Twitter, Jacobs has noticed that his anxiety has subsided and he has more time to spend on other areas of his life.

Lower Self-Esteem

A lot of people can relate to the feeling of being insecure. Some people might not like the way they look; other people might feel insecure about where they work or how much they have achieved in school. While it is natural and even useful to feel insecure from time to time, spending time on social media can amplify these insecurities. Scrolling through perfect Instagram photos or updates about others' fantastic achievements can make social media users feel like their life is messy, not working, or otherwise inadequate. According to a 2017 survey of social media sites by the United Kingdom's Royal Society for Public Health, Instagram ranked the worst for mental health. One survey participant wrote, "Instagram easily makes girls and women feel as if their bodies aren't good enough as people add filters and edit their pictures in order for them to look 'perfect.'"[39] A different study of one thousand Swedish Facebook users found similar results: women who spent more time on Facebook reported having lower self-esteem and feeling less confident. "When Facebook users compare their own lives with others' seemingly more successful careers and happy relationships, they may feel that their own lives are less successful in comparison,"[40] write the researchers.

Juliann Rasanayagam, a registered psychotherapist, knows how damaging social media can be to one's self-esteem. As a young woman, she had an account on every major social media platform. She was earning her master's degree and living at her parents' house, and it made her feel very insecure to see peers on social media who seemed further along in their careers or had already bought their own homes. "I was already feeling down on myself and my exposure to social media made this worse," she says. Every time she went on social media, she couldn't help comparing her life to her friends' lives and feeling like she wasn't keeping up with them. When she recognized how bad this made her feel, she decided to remove herself from several social media sites. She went through her accounts and cut out the ones that made her feel bad. "It turned out to be a great decision because I was no longer comparing myself and it left my self-esteem intact."[41]

> "I was already feeling down on myself and my exposure to social media made this worse."[41]
>
> —Juliann Rasanayagam, a registered psychotherapist and social media user

Taking a Toll on the Body

Being addicted to social media does more than impact a person's mental health; it also affects them physically. People who are constantly on social media suffer from carpal tunnel syndrome, which is when a compressed nerve in the wrist causes pain and numbness in the hand. They are also at risk for developing finger tendon strains caused by too much typing. Others develop problems like trigger thumb, a condition that causes pain and stiffness when bending or straightening the thumb, or thumb arthritis from too much texting and typing on smartphones. Some experience back and neck pain from being hunched over a phone or computer.

Staring at screens can also cause eyestrain, dry eyes, and blurry vision. Those who stare at screens for too many hours can permanently damage their eyes. In 2018 researchers at the Uni-

Being consumed by social media can affect a person's ability to sleep. People who have trouble turning off their thoughts might be more prone to waking up in the middle of the night to check for updates.

versity of Toledo in Ohio found that the blue light emitted by smartphones and other screens can increase one's risk of developing macular degeneration, the leading cause of vision loss. "It's no secret that blue light harms our vision by damaging the eye's retina,"[42] says study coauthor Ajith Karunarathne. Unlike other types of light, the blue light emitted by screens is dangerous because the eye's cornea and lens cannot block or reflect it. The light travels straight to light-sensitive cells in the eye's retina known as photoreceptors. When photoreceptors become overwhelmed from constant exposure to screen light, they can produce a toxic chemical that can, in turn, cause macular degeneration and even blindness. "Photoreceptor cells do not regenerate in the eye," says Kasun Ratnayake, a doctoral student who worked on the study. "When they're dead, they're dead for good."[43]

Being consumed with social media can also worsen a person's ability to sleep well. People who have trouble turning off their thoughts may be more prone to waking up in the middle of the night to check social media. A 2016 study by researchers at the University of Pittsburgh found that young adults who spend a lot of time on social media were more likely to suffer sleep disturbances than peers who used social media less. "This is one of the first pieces of evidence that social media use really can impact your sleep," says lead study author Jessica C. Levenson. In addition, the researchers found that how often a person checked social media also affected their sleep habits. Participants who most frequently checked social media throughout the week were three times more likely to have sleep disturbances, compared to those who checked the least. "This may indicate that frequency of social media visits is a better predictor of sleep difficulty than overall time spent on social media," explains Levenson. "If this is the case, then interventions that counter obsessive 'checking' behavior may be most effective."[44]

> "Social media use really can impact your sleep."[44]
>
> —Jessica C. Levenson, a researcher at the University of Pittsburgh

Damaging Relationships

Some people are so strongly drawn to social media that they have serious difficulty pulling their attention back toward where it is truly needed, which is the real world and their relationships with family and friends. Neglecting real-world relationships is something that Perri Ormont Blumberg learned about firsthand. Increasingly, when Blumberg hung out with her best friend Allie, she felt like she was competing with social media for Allie's attention. For example, when the two friends would meet for dinner, Blumberg felt like Allie paid more attention to her phone than to her. "It made me feel like I was wasting my time trying to hang out with her, and I struggled with how to approach her about it,"[45] says Blumberg. At a Bruce Springsteen concert, Blumberg remembers that Allie was more concerned about capturing everything for social media than actually enjoying the show. Even on the train ride home, Allie created taglines for her Snapchats, edited photos for an Instagram post, and scrolled through her online friends' stories on Snapchat. Every so often, she would look up from her phone to see if they had arrived at their station. Then she would go right back to her phone.

Eventually, Blumberg decided that she needed to have a serious talk with her friend and they agreed to put down the phones when they were together. "I care about Allie deeply. She's warm, funny, genuine and all-around amazing—but when she's glued to her phone 23/7, I'm pretty sure those aren't the vibes she exudes,"[46] says Blumberg.

Spiraling Out of Control

Sometimes an addiction to social media can cause a person's life to spiral out of control. When Brooke was twelve years old, she received her own smartphone. She quickly became obsessed with social media. With her phone constantly at her fingertips, she immediately answered Snapchats and FaceTime calls and waited for each reply. She spent hours on the phone, from the time

Some people are so strongly drawn to social media that they are often oblivious to the real world. This causes their relationships with family and friends to suffer.

she got home from school until she went to bed, and sometimes throughout the night. "I'd stay up until like 4:30 in the morning," she says. "I couldn't put it down. . . . It felt like a part of me."[47]

Brooke's parents tried taking away her phone, but this only caused Brooke to argue with her parents. When they tried to cut her access to social media, Brooke found ways to get around the limitations they imposed. "I was constantly making different accounts," she says. "I had like six accounts on Instagram. I had multiple Snapchats. I changed the usernames, the passwords. I would block [my parents]. I'd have other friends give me their old phones, iPods, anything, and I always had a backup ready to go,"[48] says Brooke. Brooke and her parents constantly fought about her phone use, driving a tremendous wedge into their relationship. At one point, Brooke's parents said it felt like they had no relationship with her at all, other than providing food, shelter, and a phone.

The Fear of Missing Out

One type of social anxiety triggered by social media use has become known as the fear of missing out (FOMO). FOMO is the feeling that others are having more fun, living a better life, and experiencing better things. "The FOMO experience specifically is this feeling that I personally could have been there and I wasn't," explains Amy Summerville, a psychology professor at Miami University in Ohio. It is an overwhelming frustration that one is missing out on what everyone else is doing. A person experiencing FOMO feels helpless; they think they are missing out on big, meaningful moments such as a life-changing trip, the party of the year, or meaningful gatherings with others. Of course, that is not the case; very often the experiences portrayed on social media are different from what they were like in real life. Still, FOMO is a big problem for people who are tempted to feel like they are missing out or that their experiences are not as good as those of others.

Quoted in Healthline, "The FOMO Is Real: How Social Media Increases Depression and Loneliness." www.healthline.com.

As Brooke became increasingly fixated on social media, she began to engage in risky behavior at school. At age twelve, she started drinking and using drugs. She also starting sexting with strange men that she met over social media. Some of the men convinced Brooke to send them nude photos of herself. Her parents did not know of her behavior until a police officer showed up at their door. He told her parents that Brooke and a friend were involved in a dangerous online relationship and that the person was blackmailing Brooke's friend for more nude pictures.

At school, Brooke was bullied and shamed, and she even considered suicide. At that point, her parents committed her to a residential treatment center, where as of 2017 she was being treated for several issues, including excessive use of her cell phone and social media. Periodically, she leaves the treatment center and returns home for a short visit to see how she can handle access to her cell phone and social media for a few days. Even a small thing, like being able to put on makeup without checking her phone, is a success. "For the most part, I can do things and have [my phone] in my pocket and not need it," she says. "Right now, it's not that big of an issue for me."[49]

While social media sites can have benefits, using them too frequently can lead to a variety of health and social problems. Although many people start using social media to connect and interact with others, becoming dependent on these sites can make users feel increasingly unhappy and isolated over a longer period of time.

Overcoming Social Media Addiction

When social media use turns addictive, some users decide to step away from the screen. They may quit social media entirely, but others try to slowly reduce their use. Some need the help of a professional therapist. Because addictions are highly personal, people take many different paths to overcoming their specific problem.

Digital Detox Strategies

Cell phones and other mobile devices give users access to social media anywhere there is an Internet connection or cell signal. With such easy access, social media addicts find themselves drawn into their online worlds more and more until it takes over their lives. "I used to think I was above it," says writer James Sudakow. "I would boldly profess that I didn't need to look at my phone every time a notification went off."[50]

To reduce their use of social media, some people try to detox or withdraw from the digital world. Turning off social media–related sound notifications is one way to avoid interruptions. If a person does not know that someone has messaged them or otherwise engaged with their account, it is a lot easier to avoid an interruption. Another strategy is to set self-imposed times for checking one's phone: once per hour or every few hours is reasonable. A similar approach is to set specific times of the day when social media accounts can be checked. Some people delete social media apps from their phones and mobile devices, so they are not tempted to check their social media all day long. Others leave their phones and tablets outside their bedrooms at night; this helps remove the temptation to check social media all night long.

Sudakow employed several of these strategies once he realized his social media use had become excessive. He turned off his phone's sound notifications and limited himself to checking his social media accounts once per hour. "The silence and lack of flashing was killing me," he says of the experience. After about a week, however, he became comfortable with that level of engagement, and he next limited himself to checking his social media a couple of times per day. As this became more natural, he realized that he thought about checking his accounts less and less; after a few weeks, he went the entire day without checking his accounts—he just was not thinking about them. After three weeks of practicing such habits, Sudakow was only checking his social accounts once a day. "That programmed urgency I used to exhibit before turning the notifications off to check and respond, check and respond, check and respond had subsided,"[51] he says.

After a month of practicing such behaviors, Sudakow actually went a few days without logging into social media at all—he simply forgot to check. "For the first time in a month, I wasn't being driven to the phone by the interactions themselves. I was deciding when to go in. I was in control. Not my cell phone. Not those notifications,"[52] he says. Sudakow does not plan to give up social media entirely, as he values some of the interactions he has via these platforms. Feeling in control of his use empowers him to be able to use such sites in the way they should ideally be used—for connecting with others, sharing information, and having fun.

It took an incident on vacation for Mohamed Zohny to realize that his social media use had become excessive. While at Lake Geneva in the Swiss Alps, Zohny found himself unable to relax because he was too focused on posting about every detail of

> "I would boldly profess that I didn't need to look at my phone every time a notification went off."[50]
>
> —James Sudakow, social media user

his day. Yet Zohny realized that quitting cold turkey would not be a good option for him. "At a time where data and algorithms are changing the world, I don't think quitting is the solution — especially if you work in social media or need to use it to support a business," he says. Instead, Zohny took several steps to help him reduce but not eliminate his social media use. One particularly helpful strategy was to make a note of every time he went to a social media site, logging what he did on it, and otherwise gathering detailed data about his use. "I keep track so I can see every day, how many hours . . . I actually spend," he says. "Once you start keeping score, you can decide how much time you actually want to spend consuming content." Zohny employed another strategy

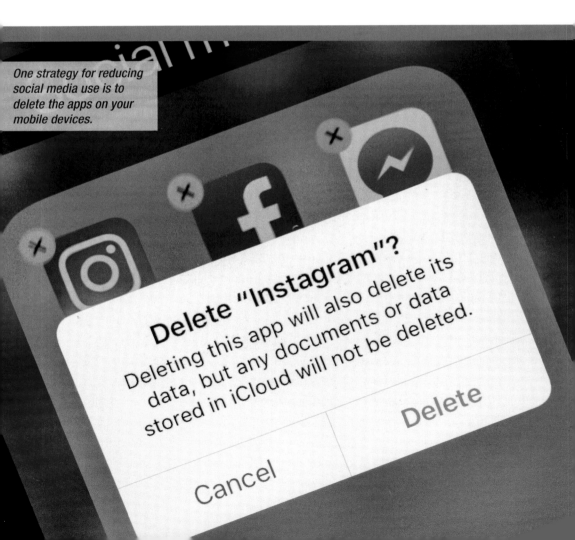

One strategy for reducing social media use is to delete the apps on your mobile devices.

Delete "Instagram"?

Deleting this app will also delete its data, but any documents or data stored in iCloud will not be deleted.

Cancel

Delete

to limit his use of social media: instead of posting photos immediately, he waited until later—after the event or trip or meal—to post them. "It's okay," he says. "Your friends will survive if they can't see it until tomorrow. When I started giving myself daily cut-off times and stopped posting in real time, I managed to reduce my social media use,"[53] he says. By delaying his posts, Zohny also says he had more time to edit them, which resulted in higher-quality posts.

"When I started giving myself daily cut-off times and stopped posting in real time, I managed to reduce my social media use."[53]

—Mohamed Zohny, social media user

Quitting Cold Turkey

Strategies that help users cut back on their social media use do not work for all people who are addicted, however. Some find it easier to close their accounts and quit using social media entirely. Steve Schlafman is one such person. In 2016, he was feeling overwhelmed by many aspects of life. "I knew I badly needed to reduce clutter and distractions from my daily routine," he says. To get a handle on how he used his time, he spent several days tracking his activities and noting which of them caused stress and anxiety. Schlafman realized that the two to three hours of time he was spending on social media was a source of stress. Whenever he had a free minute, he would check Twitter, Facebook, or Instagram. "I was constantly checking my feeds throughout the day," he says. "I'd constantly be thinking about my next post, stopping to capture that perfect picture, or ignoring whoever I was with. Worst of all, I realized social media was a vehicle to feed my ego, escape reality and flood my brain with quick bursts of dopamine."[54]

Schlafman decided to go on a digital detox and quit all social media for a month. He deleted tempting apps from his phone and logged his computer out of his social media accounts. The first few days were challenging for Schlafman; he felt bored, disconnected, depressed, and worried he was missing out. He remembers having to stick with it and give himself pep talks. "While my brain was craving that sweet burst of dopamine from online interactions, I continued to remind myself that these withdrawals would likely subside after the first week,"[55] he says.

A week into quitting cold turkey, Schlafman's anxiety and cravings for social media began to fade. He still felt disconnected and worried about missing out, but he did not feel that urgent need to go online. Instead, he put effort into having face-to-face conversations and making phone calls. After a couple weeks, he felt he had been profoundly changed. "I was much more present. My anxiety completely disappeared. I stopped thinking in tweets and visualizing photos to post. I had developed a fresher mind. I stopped comparing myself to others. I no longer felt the desire to reach for my phone throughout the day."[56] By his third week without social media, Schlafman realized that he no longer had to go online to validate his ideas and pictures or to feel funny, smart, or creative. He felt free from social media.

By the end of the month, Schlafman had made many positive changes and felt ready to return to using social media, though this time in a much more responsible and measured way. He used what he had learned about being addicted to social media to develop a healthier relationship with his online world. This is challenging, but he is making good progress and is trying to build good habits and keep his social media usage under control.

Professional Help

Some social media addicts are turning to professionals for treatment. Demand for these services is rising, and there are several types of treatment available. Some therapists offer hourly counseling sessions. Mindfulness coaches host digital detox retreats,

and corporate wellness companies strive to help users break the habit of compulsive scrolling. All are connected by the fact that they try to teach people how to develop responsible, healthy relationships with social media and the Internet.

Pamela Rutledge, the director of the Media Psychology Research Center in California, thinks part of the problem is that many people do not know how to use social media; they were never taught these skills. Social media—along with the whole of the Internet—is an enormous, often overwhelming space. However, not many schools spend time teaching students how to responsibly navigate or develop a healthy relationship with it. Indeed, in many classrooms, these skills are not formally taught, but perhaps they should be. "We give people driving lessons and swimming lessons, but everyone just gets a smartphone and off they go," says Rutledge. However, Rutledge and others think such

Going to Rehab

Some people seeking to break their addiction to social media may benefit from being treated at an in-patient rehabilitation program. In California, the Paradigm Malibu teen treatment center offers an intensive program lasting thirty to forty-five days that includes therapy and outdoor activities to help teens step away from social media. In individual and group therapy sessions, counselors help teens become aware of their addiction, understand its effects on their lives, and figure out what triggers may have contributed to their addiction. Teens can also participate in a number of other therapeutic activities including dance, art, writing, surfing, and therapy that involves horses. No cell phone use or Internet surfing is allowed while patients are in the program. According to the center, its program has an 80 percent success rate.

Seventeen-year-old Caitlyn Walker from Arizona is one person who has sought treatment at Paradigm Malibu for her nearly crippling addiction to social media. After thirty days in the program, she is not ready to completely give up social media. However, she thinks she has learned to use it in a healthier way. She also now realizes she has the power to block someone, delete them, or avoid social media entirely if it makes her feel bad.

education would be useful in the same way that it is useful for people to learn how to behave politely, eat meals with others, or otherwise follow the rules, spoken and unspoken, presented by social situations. "There are skills needed to navigate any social space,"[57] says Rutledge.

From this perspective, addiction treatments aim to help people build skills to use social media more positively, productively, and responsibly. One of the most successful types of treatments in this regard is cognitive behavioral therapy (CBT). CBT is a type of talk therapy that helps people change the way they think and behave. The goal is to help a person feel more control over his or her online activity rather than completely quit social media. A therapist teaches the patient how to recognize situations and emotions that have created problems with social media use in the past so he or she can change behavior in the future. Nathan Driskell, a therapist in Houston, Texas, who offers CBT to his patients, says that patients seeking help for social media addiction now make up almost half of his clients. Driskell works with patients in one-on-one weekly therapy sessions for at least six months to a year to help them overcome their addiction.

Although many therapists treat patients in person, a New York–based start-up company, Talkspace, is taking a different approach. It offers a twelve-week online counseling program to help those who struggle with online addictions. Therapists work with patients to increase mindfulness, and they track their progress over several months. According to Linda Sacco, Talkspace's vice president for behavioral health services, many patients turn to therapy when they have failed to control their social media impulses on the their own.

Some professionals are skeptical that online therapy like that offered by Talkspace can be as effective as in-person sessions. They say that nothing can replace the personal relationship that is developed between a therapist and patient who meet face-to-face. Another concern is the anonymity of online therapy. Without knowing a patient's identity or contact information, online therapists have no way to help patients who may be a danger to themselves or others. Still another concern is the quality of online therapists. "Not all online counseling sites use professionally trained therapists or adhere to an ethics policy,"[58] says Stephen Buckley, the head of information at Mind, a mental health charity in England.

Despite these concerns, there is hope that online therapy can open doors for people who need help but may be reluctant to more actively seek it. As technology becomes a greater part of mental health services, more research is needed to determine just how effective online therapy can be for a variety of mental health issues, including social media addiction. "There are a number of studies looking at telemedicine for different kinds of disorders and they tend to be amazingly effective,"[59] says Mary

Therapy can help patients recognize situations and emotions that have created problems with social media use. Once those issues are identified, people can try to change the way they use social media.

Ann Dutton, a professor and vice chair for research in Georgetown University Medical Center's psychology department.

Social Media Companies Are Changing Their Sites

Social media companies are beginning to recognize their role in the problem of social media addiction. This is partly why Facebook and Instagram announced in 2018 that they were launching new features that help users manage the time they spend on their sites. An activity dashboard tracks details of a user's time over the week, and a daily usage reminder makes note of when they reach their maximum allotted use (to be set by each user). Users can also now mute their push notifications for short periods of time; this can help cut down on interruptions. "We developed these tools based on collaboration and inspiration from leading mental health experts and organizations, academics, our own extensive research and feedback from our community," said the companies in a joint statement. "We want the time people spend on Facebook and Instagram to be intentional, positive and inspiring. Our hope is that these tools give people more control over the time they spend on our platforms and also foster conversations between parents and teens about the online habits that are right for them."[60]

However, critics warn that these efforts may be missing the mark in terms of meaningfully responding to the serious problem of social media addiction. One problem is that these tools do not differentiate between active and passive site use. Active use is

Boundless Mind's Space App

Interestingly, and perhaps ironically, some people are turning to an app to help them break their addiction to social media. A company called Boundless Mind has created the app, which is called Space. After users install Space on their phones, they pick a social media site (such as Pinterest or WhatsApp) that they want to use less often. The Space app walks the user through linking Facebook (or any other social media site they choose) to Space, replacing Facebook's icon on the phone's home screen with a Space version of it.

When the user wants to check Facebook, they have to click the new Space icon on their phone. When the app opens, a calming prompt appears and instructs them to take two deep breaths. After a short time, the Space app opens Facebook. This delay breaks the instant gratification that users get when they click the Facebook app on their phone, which helps them better manage their social media use. "That little delay, that little moment of Zen, helps rewire the instant gratification sensors in your brain to not make you want to go out and impulsively check Instagram or binge on Twitter," says Matthew Mayberry, a behavior designer from Boundless Mind.

Quoted in Tom Haberstroh, "Is Social Media Addiction in the NBA Out of Control?," Bleacher Report, October 1, 2018. https://bleacherreport.com.

when someone comments on photos or engages with others; passive use is when someone, say, scrolls through feeds, reading content but not interacting with others. It is the passive use that is particularly problematic in terms of social media addiction, and it is more meaningful to track. "You can't tell active and passive Facebooking apart from the dashboard," says Josh Constine, a technology journalist who specializes in social networks. "There's no way to see a breakdown of how long you spend browsing the News Feed, watching Stories or exploring photos on profiles versus creating posts or comments, messaging or interacting in Groups. That segmentation would give users a much clearer view of where they're spending or wasting hours, and what they could do to make their usage healthier."[61]

When it comes to addressing social media addiction, there is no one solution that works for everyone. Whereas some people are able to find success using digital detox strategies, others find it better to sign off from social media entirely. Social media companies also have a role to play in helping people use their platforms in responsible, healthy, and productive ways. It is clear that social media is a powerful technology that is here to stay. Therefore, it is increasingly important for people to be careful about how they use these emerging platforms and to learn to set reasonable limits for their use.

Introduction: Looking for Likes

1. Elizabeth Stinson, "Stop the Endless Scroll. Delete Social Media from Your Phone," *Wired*, October 1, 2017. www.wired.com.
2. Hayley Sewell, "My Social Media Addiction Took Over My Life," BusinessCloud.com, February 4, 2019. www.businesscloud.co.uk.

Chapter One: What Does It Mean to Be Addicted to Social Media?

3. Samantha Matt, "My Addiction to Social Media Is Killing Me," *Seventeen*, June 30, 2015. www.seventeen.com/life/real-girl-stories/a31993/my-addiction-to-social-media-is-killing-me.
4. Matt, "My Addiction to Social Media Is Killing Me."
5. Cecilie Schou Andreassen, Ståle Pallesen, and Mark D. Griffiths, "The Relationship Between Addictive Use of Social Media, Narcissism, and Self-Esteem: Findings from a Large National Survey," *Addictive Behaviors*, January 2017, vol. 64, pp. 287–93.
6. Quoted in Carolyn Gregoire, "Research Links Addictive Social Media Behavior with Substance Abuse," *Huffington Post*, December 13, 2014. www.huffingtonpost.com.
7. Quoted in Sophia Smith Galer, "How Much Is 'Too Much Time' on Social Media?," BBC, January 19, 2018. www.bbc.com.
8. Quoted in Swansea University, "Internet Withdrawal Increases Heart Rate and Blood Pressure: Scientists Find That Internet Withdrawal Increases Heart Rate and Blood Pressure," ScienceDaily, May 31, 2017. www.sciencedaily.com.

9. Quoted in Swansea University, "Internet Withdrawal Increases Heart Rate and Blood Pressure."

10. Quoted in MSU Today, "Excessive Social Media Use Is Comparable to Drug Addiction," January 10, 2019. https://msu today.msu.edu.

11. Quoted in MSU Today, "Excessive Social Media Use Is Comparable to Drug Addiction."

12. Jason Thibeault, "Why I Just Quit Facebook," LinkedIn, August 21, 2014. www.linkedin.com.

Chapter Two: Why Is Social Media So Addictive?

13. Quoted in Stuart Wolpart, "UCLA Neuroscientist's Book Explains Why Social Connection Is as Important as Food and Shelter," UCLA Newsroom, October 10, 2013. http://news room.ucla.edu.

14. Quoted in Catharine Price, "Trapped—the Secret Ways Social Media Is Built to Be Addictive (and What You Can Do to Fight Back)," Science Focus, October 29, 2018. www.science focus.com.

15. Quoted in Simon Parkin, "Has Dopamine Got Us Hooked on Tech?," *Guardian* (Manchester, UK), March 4, 2018. www .theguardian.com.

16. Quoted in Susie East, "Teens: This Is How Social Media Affects Your Brain," CNN, August 1, 2016. www.cnn.com.

17. Quoted in Natalie Jacewicz, "Social Media Is Harming Our Youth, Right? Maybe Not," *Tampa Bay (FL) Times*, October 12, 2017. www.tampabay.com.

18. Quoted in BBC, "FOMO: How the Fear of Missing Out Drives Social Media 'Addiction,'" March 1, 2017. www.bbc.com.

19. Quoted in Julian Morgans, "Your Addiction to Social Media Is No Accident," Vice, May 19, 2017. www.vice.com.

20. Quoted in Hilary Andersson, "Social Media Apps Are 'Deliberately' Addictive to Users," BBC, July 4, 2018. www.bbc.com.

21. Quoted in Morgans, "Your Addiction to Social Media Is No Accident."
22. Quoted in Morgans, "Your Addiction to Social Media Is No Accident."
23. Quoted in Andersson, "Social Media Apps Are 'Deliberately' Addictive to Users."
24. Quoted in Andersson, "Social Media Apps Are 'Deliberately' Addictive to Users."
25. Quoted in Andersson, "Social Media Apps Are 'Deliberately' Addictive to Users."

Chapter Three: How Do People Become Addicted to Social Media?

26. Hattie Gladwell, "How My Addiction to Social Media Affected My Mental Health and My Relationships," Metro News, September 5, 2017. https://metro.co.uk.
27. Gladwell, "How My Addiction to Social Media Affected My Mental Health and My Relationships."
28. Gladwell, "How My Addiction to Social Media Affected My Mental Health and My Relationships."
29. Quoted in Galer, "How Much Is 'Too Much Time' on Social Media?"
30. Anonymous, "Why Social Media and My Addictive Personality Don't Mesh," Tiny Buddha (blog). https://tinybuddha.com.
31. Anonymous, "Why Social Media and My Addictive Personality Don't Mesh."
32. Quoted in Tim Newman, "Unlocking the Personality of a Social Media Addict," Medical News Today, March 17, 2018. www.medicalnewstoday.com.
33. Quoted in David Nield, "These Are the Personality Traits That Could Get You Addicted to Social Media," Science Alert, March 17, 2018. www.sciencealert.com.

Chapter Four: Living with a Social Media Addiction

34. L.Y. Lin et al., "Association Between Social Media Use and Depression Among U.S. Young Adults," *Depression and Anxiety*, 2016, vol. 33, no. 4, pp. 323–31.

35. Quoted in Alice Walton, "New Studies Show Just How Bad Social Media Is for Mental Health," *Forbes*, November 16, 2018. www.forbes.com.

36. Jennifer Garam, "Social Media Makes Me Feel Bad About Myself," *Progress Not Perfection* (blog), *Psychology Today*, September 26, 2011. www.psychologytoday.com.

37. Quoted in Andersson, "Social Media Apps Are 'Deliberately' Addictive to Users."

38. Quoted in Sabrina Barr, "Six Ways Social Media Negativity Affects Your Mental Health," *Independent* (London), January 28, 2019. www.independent.co.uk.

39. Quoted in Amanda MacMillan, "Why Instagram Is the Worst Social Media Network for Mental Health," *Time*, May 25, 2017. http://time.com.

40. Quoted in Jessica Brown, "Is Social Media Bad for You? The Evidence and the Unknowns," BBC, January 5, 2018. www .bbc.com.

41. Quoted in Taylor Bennett, "Why Social Media Makes You Sad," Thriveworks, June 15, 2018. https://thriveworks.com.

42. Quoted in Hannah Sparks, "Your Phone Is Blinding You, Scientists Warn," *New York Post*, August 13, 2018. https://ny post.com.

43. Quoted in Sparks, "Your Phone Is Blinding You, Scientists Warn."

44. Quoted in University of Pittsburgh Schools of the Health Sciences, "Social Media Use in Young Adults Linked to Sleep Disturbance," ScienceDaily, January 26, 2016. www.science daily.com.

45. Perri Ormont Blumberg, "My Best Friend Is a Social Media Addict—Here's How I Dealt with It," *Glamour*, September 20, 2016. www.glamour.com.

46. Blumberg, "My Best Friend Is a Social Media Addict."

47. Quoted in Eric M. Strauss, "How This Teen Fell into a World of Sexting, Alcohol, and Drugs," ABC News, May 16, 2017. https://abcnews.go.com.

48. Quoted in Strauss, "How This Teen Fell into a World of Sexting, Alcohol, and Drugs."

49. Quoted in Strauss, "How This Teen Fell into a World of Sexting, Alcohol, and Drugs."

Chapter Five: Overcoming Social Media Addiction

50. James Sudakow, "I Turned Off All of My Social Media Notifications for a Month, and I Lived to Tell the Tale," *Inc.*, August 22, 2018. www.inc.com.

51. Sudakow, "I Turned Off All of My Social Media Notifications for a Month, and I Lived to Tell the Tale."

52. Sudakow, "I Turned Off All of My Social Media Notifications for a Month, and I Lived to Tell the Tale."

53. Mohamed Zohny, "How I Reduced My Social Media Addiction Without Going Cold Turkey," Medium, July 16, 2018. https://medium.com.

54. Steve Schlafman, "I Am a Social Media Addict and I Quit for a Month. Here's My Story," Medium, August 8, 2016. https://medium.com.

55. Schlafman, "I Am a Social Media Addict and I Quit for a Month."

56. Schlafman, "I Am a Social Media Addict and I Quit for a Month."

57. Quoted in Alina Dizik, "The Addiction That's 'Worse than Alcohol or Drug Abuse,'" BBC, April 18, 2017. www.bbc.com.

58. Quoted in Rebecca Ratcliffe, "Thousands Go Online for Therapy. But Does It Work?," *Guardian* (Manchester, UK), February 12, 2017. www.theguardian.com.
59. Quoted in Allison Fox, "Does Online Therapy Actually Work?," *Huffington Post*, March 1, 2017. www.huffpost.com.
60. Ameet Ranadive and David Ginsberg, "New Tools to Manage Your Time on Facebook and Instagram," Facebook Newsroom, August 1, 2018. https://newsroom.fb.com.
61. Josh Constine, "Facebook Is Finally Rolling Out Its 'How Long Do I Spend on Facebook,'" TechCrunch, November 20, 2018. https://techcrunch.com.

American Psychological Association
750 First St. NE
Washington, DC 20002
website: www.apa.org

The American Psychological Association represents American psychologists who study and treat human behavior. Its website features information about psychology topics, including addiction, and contains links to many publications.

Common Sense Media
650 Townsend St., Suite 435
San Francisco, CA 94103
website: www.commonsensemedia.org

Common Sense Media is a nonprofit organization dedicated to helping kids and parents use technology and media, including social media, in a responsible way. The site has links to research and articles for families about social media use in the United States.

ConnectSafely
website: www.connectsafely.org

ConnectSafely is committed to educating users about how to get the most from their technology, including social networks, while being responsible and safe. The site has tips for teens and resources for safe blogging and social media.

Internet and Technology Addicts Anonymous (ITAA)
website: https://internetaddictsanonymous.org

The ITAA is a twelve-step program and support group for people with Internet and technology addictions, including social media addictions. The website provides information about local meetings and online support groups.

Pew Research Center
1615 L St. NW, Suite 800
Washington, DC 20036
website: www.pewresearch.org

The Pew Research Center is a think tank that conducts research, public opinion polls, demographic research, and other social science research to inform the public about the issues and trends shaping today's world, including Internet and social media use.

Books

Barbara Gottfried Hollander, *I Am a Digital Addict, Now What?* New York: Rosen, 2017.

Jack Lasky, *The Internet*. Farmington Hills, MI: Greenhaven, 2016.

Andrea C. Nakaya, *Internet and Social Media Addiction*. San Diego: ReferencePoint, 2015.

Patricia Netzley, *Online Addiction*. San Diego: ReferencePoint, 2017.

Jackson Nieuwland, *Coping with Social Media Anxiety*. New York: Rosen, 2018.

Peggy J. Parks, *Social Media*. San Diego: ReferencePoint, 2017.

Laura Perdew, *Internet Addiction*. Minneapolis: ABDO, 2015.

Internet Sources

Monica Anderson and Jingjing Jiang, "Teens' Social Media Habits and Experiences," Pew Research Center, November 28, 2018. www.pewinternet.org.

Benedict Carey, "This Is Your Brain Off Facebook," *New York Times*, January 30, 2019. www.nytimes.com.

Common Sense Media, "2018 Social Media, Social Life." www.commonsensemedia.org.

Pew Research Center, "Social Media Use in 2018," March 1, 2018. www.pewinternet.org.

Catharine Price, "Trapped—the Secret Ways Social Media Is Built to Be Addictive (and What You Can Do to Fight Back)," Science Focus, October 29, 2018. www.sciencefocus.com.

Kevin Roose, "Do Not Disturb: How I Ditched My Phone and Un-broke My Brain," *New York Times*, February 23, 2019. www.ny times.com.

Lauren Sharkey, "Is Social Media Addiction a Disorder? Re-searchers Think the Problem Needs to Be Taken More Seriously," *Bustle*, January 12, 2019. www.bustle.com.

Nitasha Tiku, "The Wired Guide to Internet Addiction," *Wired*, April 18, 2018. www.wired.com.

Picture Credits

Cover: Mixmike/iStockphoto.com

6: Maury Aaseng

10: Antonio Guillem/Shutterstock.com

13: Grigorev_Vladimir/iStockphoto.com

16: fizkes/Shutterstock.com

21: Rawpixel.com/Shutterstock.com

23: Andrii Vodalazhskyi/Shutterstock.com

27: Hadrian/Shutterstock.com

32: Nejron Photo/Shutterstock.com

35: threerocksimages/Shutterstock.com

38: Kaspars Grinvalds/Shutterstock.com

43: Antonio Guillem/Shutterstock.com

46: nito/Shutterstock.com

49: Antonio Guillem/Shutterstock.com

54: Ink Drop/Shutterstock.com

57: Dean Drobot/Shutterstock.com

60: Photographee.eu/Shutterstock.com

Carla Mooney is the author of many books for young adults and children. She lives in Pittsburgh, Pennsylvania, with her husband and three children, and she enjoys learning about issues that affect today's teens.